ORIGINAL SOUND

Adam Seidel

BROADWAY PLAY PUBLISHING INC
New York
www.broadwayplaypub.com
info@broadwayplaypub.com

Cover photo by Adam Seidel

First edition: November 2020
I S B N: 978-0-88145-859-6

Book design: Marie Donovan
Page make-up: Adobe InDesign
Typeface: Palatino

The world premiere of ORIGINAL SOUND was produced by Cherry Lane Alternative (General Manager, Julie Crosby), opening on 9 May 2019 and closing on 8 June. The cast and creative contributors were:

RYAN REED...Jane Bruce
DANNY SOLIS ....Sebastian Chacon
KARI RIVER..Lio Mehiel
FELICIA SOLIS ....Cynthia Bastidas
JAKE COLBURN...Anthony Arkin
TOMMY SOLIS............................ Wilson Jermaine Heredia

Director... Elena Araoz
Assistant director.. Kristin Rion
Musical director... Daniel Ocanto
Set design...Justin Townsend
Lighting design .... Kate McGee
Costumes..Sarita Fellows
Sound design... Nathan Leigh
Props .... Lauren Page Russel
Stage manager.. Christine Lemme
Assistant stage manager ....Carolyn Reich

The author would like to give a special thank you to Pulse Ensemble Theatre Playwrights Lab, which the play was part of in 2018.

CHARACTERS & SETTING

DANNY SOLIS (*sol-ees*), *Latino, D J/musician, 22, M*
FELICIA SOLIS, *Latina, nurse,* DANNY'*s sister, 34, F*
KARI RIVER, DANNY'*s friend, music fan, 22, N-B*
RYAN REED, *Caucasian pop music artist, 24, F*
JAKE COLBURN, RYAN'*s manager, 50s, M*
TOMMY SOLIS, *Latino,* DANNY *and* FELICIA'*s dad, 48, M*

Set design should not bog down the speed of the play. One scene should flow into another quickly.

Thoughts on sound design for transitions: Transitions for this play can either be hip hop that's totally current to 2016 or they can be songs played simultaneously, two or three on top of each other. They can work together well or not work at all.

I strongly encourage producers to use the music created for the world premiere because it's dope. This sheet music may be purchased and downloaded from www.broadwayplaypub.com.

A NOTE ON SCENES

Scenes 8 and 14 were written following the Cherry Lane production. The play can be performed with or without them.

Like they say,
every dog has its day
and like they say
God works in a mysterious way.

Keith Edward Elam (Gang Starr)

Prologue

(A sound booth in a high end recording studio. RYAN, *24, enters and walks to a music stand with an acoustic guitar. She puts on headphones.)*

RYAN: Can you hear me? So this is a new song. It's kinda rough. You ready? *(She plays a song, singing with edge, heart and soul.)*
I'm saying goodbye in my head
While you and I still lay in bed
I know you know I plan to leave
Should I wear black so you can start to grieve
Can I stay away?

You've been livin in my wounds for too long
Stop cryin I just need you gone
You dug your claws in once before
What makes you think I'd give you anymore

We're like a car crash on a starry night
I know I should buckle up but I think I like the fight
I'm addicted to your trouble and you feel so right

I should stay away
I crawl back anyway
I can't stay away
I stay

My memories should be enough
But you know how I like it rough
So come on in I'll pour the wine
And remind you that you're mine
I can't stay away

Maybe fairytales are true
But I think I'd rather hurt with you
I know my mom would shake her head
But I've never listened to a word she said

We're like a car crash on a starry night
I know I should buckle up but I think I like the fight
I'm addicted to your trouble and you feel so right

I should stay away
I crawl back anyway
I can't stay away
I stay

When you left I thought I'd be fine
I found my footing every other time
But your danger is my favorite kind
Who cares if I lose my mind

We're like a car crash on a starry night
I know I should buckle up but I think I like the fight
I'm addicted to your trouble and you feel so right
We're a toxic combination that I can't explain
Baby how you burn so good I like it and I can't
    complain
I'm laying on the tracks waiting for your train
I know this love might kill me but I'm not afraid
Maybe I deserve it I'm a bad girl time my debt got
    paid.
I've been dreaming for too long I'm drowning in this
bed I've made

I should stay away
I crawl back anyway
I can't stay away
I stay
(She finishes the song.) What do you think?

Scene 1

(An apartment in Queens. Sparse, not broke ass. DANNY, *22, sits wearing headphones working on something on his computer, we see him nodding his head to a beat, which we can faintly hear. He's into what he's working on.)*

(There's a loud knock on the door.)

(A louder knock on the door.)

*(*DANNY *goes to the door and opens it.)*

*(*FELICIA, *his older sister, mid 30s, enters.)*

DANNY: Thought you were stopping by last night.

FELICIA: You didn't text me your address.

DANNY: Yeah I did.

FELICIA: When I was already at work.

DANNY: I got busy with stuff.

FELICIA: Explain how you get too busy to send a text.

DANNY: The point is you're here now.

FELICIA: So how was work today?

DANNY: Work was, work.

FELICIA: Really? Cause I got a call from Ron. You know what he told me? That he fired you this morning.

DANNY: He didn't fire me. I quit.

FELICIA: He said you told him to stick a broom handle up his ass.

DANNY: Because the guy orders me around like he's my dad.

FELICIA: He is your dad.

DANNY: He's my step dad.

FELICIA: I'm not getting into a debate about this. Tomorrow you're going back to that restaurant and getting your job back.

DANNY: It's a menial job serving shitty Mexican food.

FELICIA: Well it gives mom the impression you're not wasting your damn life.

DANNY: Ma put you up to this, didn't she?

FELICIA: Actually she doesn't know yet, so fix this before she does.

DANNY: What's she gonna do? Yell at me?

FELICIA: No. She's going to come over to my house and unload on me. And as much as I love being mom's go to for emotional support I'm too damn busy.

DANNY: So this visit is a pre-emptive strike?

FELICIA: This visit is me making sure that your ass is okay.

DANNY: I am okay!

FELICIA: You don't look okay. I mean for starters what's up with those clothes?

DANNY: My threads are fly.

FELICIA: Really? Cause to me you look like one of those guys who stand next to A T Ms and beg for money.

DANNY: Those guys actually make a lot of money doing that.

FELICIA: …

DANNY: Dude, get off my ass!

FELICIA: I'll get off your ass when you stop acting like an idiot.

DANNY: You did the exact same shit when you were my age.

FELICIA: I never told anyone to shove a broom up their ass.

DANNY: I meant you moving out of ma's.

FELICIA: I was getting married.

DANNY: And you were pregnant.

FELICIA: Quiere que te meto un puno?! *(You want to get hit?)*

DANNY: I'm not sayin' it's bad. I'm just sayin'.

(Beat. FELICIA picks up her purse and takes out her wallet.)

FELICIA: Do you have money?

DANNY: Yeah.

FELICIA: Do I want to know how you got it?

DANNY: Probably not.

(FELICIA throws her wallet back in her purse.)

FELICIA: Danny, help me understand what's going on with you.

DANNY: I'm just done being around people who hate on my shit.

FELICIA: What shit?

DANNY: My music.

FELICIA: Danny—

DANNY: Don't start. I'm committed to it, I'm doing it, and that's that.

FELICIA: You know, you've never played me any of your stuff.

DANNY: You never asked.

FELICIA: So play me something now.

DANNY: That's okay.

FELICIA: What? You scared of letting me hear it?

DANNY: No. You just wouldn't get it.

FELICIA: Hey I'm with it.

DANNY: The last time you gave me a lift somewhere you were listening to Michael Buble.

FELICIA: Just play me something.

(Beat. Then DANNY *opens the computer.)*

DANNY: So, this is my music page.

FELICIA: *(Reading off the screen.)* The Four Twenty Collective.

DANNY: That's my artist name.

FELICIA: Mom would love that.

DANNY: Add it to the list.

FELICIA: So what am I looking at?

DANNY: These are my tracks. And those are the comments from listeners.

FELICIA: "Your beats make my ears want to cum?"

DANNY: That's the biggest compliment I ever got.

FELICIA: What's this song "Forget Ryan Reed." That an, ex?

DANNY: No. She's this flavor-of-the-month pop singer who's blowing up. So I remixed one of her singles as a "fuck you, you suck" sort of thing.

FELICIA: "This remix is not only a dis to Ryan Reed, but to every no talent fake ass pop star out there."

DANNY: That's for people not able to pick up on the subtlety of my intention.

FELICIA: What's this other song "Sway"?

DANNY: It's just a song.

FELICIA: Let me hear it.

*(*DANNY *hands* FELICIA *headphones.)*

DANNY: Use the phones.

FELICIA: Why?

DANNY: It's the best way to hear it. Trust me.

(FELICIA *puts on the head phones.*)

FELICIA: Vale.

(DANNY *plays the track. We faintly hear it. After a moment she starts to dance, awkardly.*)

FELICIA: I like it.

DANNY: Yeah?

FELICIA: Yeah. Looks like other people do too. It's got like twenty-thousand clicks.

DANNY: For the internet that's like practically nothing.

(*The door opens and* KARI, *similar in age to* DANNY, *enters wearing a work uniform.*)

KARI: Hello.

DANNY: Oh hey Kari. You're home early.

KARI: Work was slow. Who's this?

DANNY: This is my sister.

KARI: I wasn't aware you had a sister.

FELICIA: Well he does. And you are?

KARI: The person who owns this place. Anyway, I just came back to change. (*Exits*)

FELICIA: Okay are you for real right now?

DANNY: What?

FELICIA: You're living with some girl??

DANNY: Kari's a friend.

FELICIA: A friend?

DANNY: They get what I'm about, come to my shows, dig my music.

FELICIA: So like a groupie?

DANNY: Not even close. Kari's like the most open minded person I know.

FELICIA: So why's she living in this fucked up building?

DANNY: Cause their dad owns the shit.

FELICIA: I thought she owned it.

DANNY: Same shit.

FELICIA: And she's letting you stay here why?

DANNY: Because I had nowhere else to go.

FELICIA: You can stay plenty of places.

DANNY: Not your house.

FELICIA: Who's fault is that?

DANNY: You're the one who married a herb.

FELICIA: You really want to get into it?

DANNY: I'm just sayin'.

(KARI *enters wearing new clothes.*)

KARI: Okay I'm out.

DANNY: Cool.

KARI: I'm going to this D J thing at the Beat Kitchen. You should come.

DANNY: I need to get some stuff done tonight. But maybe.

KARI: Great. *(Beat)* Nice to meet you Danny's sister.

FELICIA: Felicia.

KARI: Okay. *(Exits)*

FELICIA: So are you two like…

DANNY: What? Like together?

FELICIA: Yes.

DANNY: Yeah Felicia. We're together. We're getting married. Cause we're pregnant.

FELICIA: Okay I was just asking.

(DANNY's phone rings.)

DANNY: Shit. It's ma.

FELICIA: Might as well get it over with.

DANNY: I'll deal with it later.

(After a moment FELICIA's phone rings.)

DANNY: Don't answer it.

FELICIA: (Answering.) Hey Ma. No, I haven't talked with him. I tried but he didn't pick up. Look, I'll take care of it. Mom I need to go I'm walking through my front door love you. (Hangs up.) You happy? Now I gotta go over there next and calm her down.

DANNY: I'll handle it.

FELICIA: I gotta go.

DANNY: You just got here.

FELICIA: I need to pick up dinner. It's hamburger and spaghetti sauce night. The twins favorite.

(FELICIA gets her things together, then hugs DANNY.)

FELICIA: Portate bien. And call ma! (She leaves.)

Scene 2

(The next day. A hotel room in Manhattan. RYAN strums chords on a guitar trying to work something out. It's not going well. A knock at the door. RYAN answers it and we see JAKE, early 50s, who holds a deli paper bag.)

JAKE: Why aren't you dressed?

RYAN: We don't have to be at the studio for an hour.

JAKE: The session got moved to ten thirty.

RYAN: What?

JAKE: I sent you a text.

RYAN: I don't check texts

JAKE: Hence we're having this conversation.

RYAN: Why are we starting early?

JAKE: Because Bob needs to cut out early.

RYAN: Jesus. This is like the third time in two weeks.

JAKE: I know.

RYAN: I mean I get that Bob is such a big deal, but there is a thing called professional courtesy.

JAKE: Ryan I'm not disagreeing.

RYAN: So why does he need to cut early? Tinder date?

JAKE: Ha, no. He's catching an afternoon flight.

RYAN: To L A?

JAKE: *(He clearly knows.)* He didn't say.

RYAN: Jake just tell me what he's doing.

JAKE: He's got a meeting.

RYAN: With who?

JAKE: *(He considers a moment, then—)* Beiber.

RYAN: Justin?

JAKE: His sister, Jazmyn.

RYAN: She's like six years old.

JAKE: Eight and a half. And he's just doing a vocal demo with her and he'll be back the day after tomorrow.

RYAN: Recording this album in New York was a mistake. We should've insisted we stay in Detroit.

JAKE: Why?

RYAN: Because in Detroit I would've worked with a producer who's not an ass bag.

JAKE: Ryan do you or don't you want to break through to the top level?

RYAN: I am at the top level.

JAKE: No, you're near the top level. Which is why this album needs to be produced by Bob. Because Bob is the best.

RYAN: Is he?

JAKE: He's only produced seven Grammy- winning records.

RYAN: And he's grinding the soul out of this one! I mean look at yesterday. Forty-two takes of one chorus? If I have to sing that shit one more time I'm gonna straight up vom.

JAKE: Ryan there's no need to vom. This record is going to be good.

RYAN: But I don't want it to 'be good'. I want it to define who I am as a artist.

JAKE: On a positive note, your single that we're releasing tomorrow is going to blow the charts wide open.

RYAN: *(Exhales)* Yeah.

JAKE: I'm paying you a compliment.

RYAN: I get it. I'm just wondering, maybe we should hold off on releasing it.

JAKE: What?

RYAN: I'm just don't know if it's the right track.

JAKE: Are you fucking kidding me? I know hits and the song is a hit.

RYAN: You're right. Sorry.

JAKE: I forgive you. *(Getting a text.)* Now get your ass in gear. Our car's out front. Also, take this.

(JAKE hands RYAN the deli bag.)

RYAN: What is it?

JAKE: Beet juice. Breakfast of champions.

RYAN: It's morning, Jake. I need carbs.

JAKE: The label says ixnay on the carbs. See you downstairs. *(He exits.)*

Scene 3

(The next day in the apartment. KARI is on their way out the door, when DANNY, who is totally freaked out, flies through it.)

DANNY: Dude something happened!

KARI: What??

(DANNY starts to take his computer out of his backpack.)

DANNY: Something crazy. Like so crazy. More than crazy. Black Mirror shit.

KARI: Danny you're scaring me.

DANNY: I can't help it! I'm freaking out!

KARI: Just tell me what happened.

DANNY: This!

(The computer now open, DANNY presses a button and we hear the song RYAN was singing earlier, but with an up tempo drum beat and other added elements to give it that "pop" feel.)

KARI: What is this?

DANNY: The new Ryan Reed single.

(KARI listens a moment, then it clicks for them.)

KARI: Wait.

DANNY: Yeah.

KARI: That sounds exactly like your one track.

DANNY: Sway. I know.

(DANNY *and* KARI *both start to sway to the music.*)

KARI: The melody. The hook!

DANNY: Yep!

KARI: It just has a sped up beat and lyrics.

DANNY: Totally!

KARI: *(Looking at computer.)* Dude, she named her song *Stay*?

DANNY: She's playing games!

KARI: This has over three million plays.

DANNY: And the shit's only been out a few hours!

KARI: Danny! You wrote a hit song!

DANNY: I didn't though!

KARI: This is your music!

DANNY: But it's her lyrics! Her name! I mean is this what she does? Going around ripping off people's shit who hit her up with dis tracks? Cause I'd think she'd hit me back with a cease and desist, not this!

KARI: Danny the point is she stole your song.

DANNY: I know!

KARI: *(Turning down the music)* So what are you going to do?

DANNY: Flame her ass on Twitter and then link that shit on my Instagram.

KARI: And why would you do that?

DANNY: So I'll get noticed.

KARI: Until the next cat video blows up. Danny. Think about this. There's a ninety-nine point nine percent chance this music is yours, right?

DANNY: Right.

KARI: And anyone who hears your track next to hers will recognize that, right?

DANNY: No doubt.

KARI: So what does that mean?

DANNY: That she's fake as fuck.

KARI: It also means that Ryan Reed is in an incredibly vulnerable position. You go to the press with this and what do they do?

DANNY: Ignore me?

KARI: If we didn't have proof, yes. But we have proof.

DANNY: So you're saying I go to the press?

KARI: What I'm saying is we've got major leverage. So we need to use it.

DANNY: …

KARI: There's no way you can do this alone. It's too big and too important.

DANNY: But what do you even know about this stuff?

KARI: I know tons about music.

DANNY: But this isn't just music. This is business stuff.

KARI: I went to Columbia for business.

DANNY: But you failed out.

KARI: I dropped out.

DANNY: Is there a difference?

KARI: Dropping out was a choice.

(*A beat*)

DANNY: So what's our plan?

KARI: We contact Ryan's people and request a meeting.

DANNY: A meeting?

KARI: Yep.

DANNY: They'll just tell us to fuck off.

KARI: They won't.

DANNY: Why?

KARI: Because. We're not trying to create a problem. We're going to them to offer a solution.

Scene 4

(The next morning. RYAN's hotel room. She stands with JAKE.)

JAKE: So the kid's lying?

RYAN: I didn't say that.

JAKE: Then he's not lying?

RYAN: I don't know.

JAKE: Either the kid's lying or he's not.

RYAN: Don't paint me into a corner.

JAKE: I'm trying to understand the situation.

RYAN: There's nothing to understand. The songs are only kinda similar.

JAKE: They sound pretty fucking exactly the same to me.

RYAN: Are you a musician?

JAKE: In my twenties I played the drums.

RYAN: I meant professionally as a career. Is that what you do?

JAKE: No I'm your manager.

RYAN: Exactly! So if anyone is going to say what song sounds like what, it should be me.

JAKE: I'm trying to protect you.

RYAN: Then do that.

JAKE: I can't when you're not telling me what the fuck is going on.

RYAN: Fine I took the fucking song! You happy?!

JAKE: Absolutely not! This is a goddamn calamity.

RYAN: Big picture, is it really that big of a deal?

JAKE: The entire point of this album is that you write your own material!

RYAN: It's not like I ripped off Doctor Dre. This is just some nobody.

JAKE: Are you aware of what happens if this Four Twenty Collective kid goes to the media?

RYAN: They maybe write a story.

JAKE: You'll be painted as a fucking pariah. Then Bob drops your project, the label terminates the album.

RYAN: They're not terminating my album. I'm too big.

JAKE: Not that big.

RYAN: Stay is a hit.

JAKE: That you ripped off.

RYAN: Forget My Heart was a hit too.

JAKE: It cracked the top forty for three days.

RYAN: Who's side are you on here??

JAKE: I'm on the side that keeps your career from turning into a flaming bag of shit! Why would you do this?

RYAN: Because I was blocked and Bob was up my ass to come up with something new.

JAKE: So you stole a song.

RYAN: Okay it's not like I've ever done this before.

JAKE: Jesus. I should hope fucking not.

RYAN: I tried to tell you.

JAKE: When?

RYAN: The other day. When I was wondering if it was the right song.

JAKE: Next time try to make that a little clearer. How the hell did you even find this kid's music?

RYAN: I Googled myself.

JAKE: Excuse me?

RYAN: You don't do that?

JAKE: Hell no. I don't want to know what's out there about me.

RYAN: Well I want to know what's out there about me.

JAKE: That's what your PR team is for.

RYAN: I wanted to find out myself. And in my search I found a remix he made of "Forget My Heart" which is clearly a dis track.

JAKE: The kid made a dis track. So what??

RYAN: So it pisses me off. I mean I'm working my ass off and along comes some fucking kid who completely shits on me and what gives him the right?

JAKE: It's called the internet.

RYAN: Well the internet fucking sucks!

JAKE: You're right it does suck. It's a cruel and vicious place. But just because some kid made a dis track doesn't give you the right to take one of his songs!

RYAN: I know. But unlike every other dis track out there about me, his was actually good. So I searched through his other stuff and came across his song and it was super catchy, so in a moment of weakness and stress—I'm sorry.

JAKE: Saying sorry isn't going to fix this. You're giving the kid co-credit on the single.

RYAN: Do I have to?

JAKE: Yes.

RYAN: But how will that work?

JAKE: We slip in his name as co-writer when the album is released.

RYAN: And the label won't care?

JAKE: No because the money comes out of your end.

RYAN: Why's it coming out of my end?

JAKE: You fucking kidding me?

RYAN: Has he already agreed to this?

JAKE: Not yet, but at the meeting he will.

RYAN: What meeting?

JAKE: He wants an in-person meeting.

RYAN: There's no fucking way I'm doing that.

JAKE: I'm going on your behalf.

RYAN: Where are you meeting him?

JAKE: A restaurant in Queens.

RYAN: Why?

JAKE: Because that's where the kid lives.

RYAN: Is that a good idea?

JAKE: Are you telling me how to do my job?

RYAN: I'm just wondering if this is the best way to handle things.

JAKE: We can always go to the label and tell them you stole the song.

RYAN: Meeting with him sounds fine.

JAKE: Glad you think so. Now if you'll excuse me I've got a million phone calls to make. Have a good session with Bob. *(He turns to exit.)*

RYAN: This is going to work, right?

JAKE: Easy peasey.

(JAKE exits. RYAN exhales.)

Scene 5

(That evening. A restaurant in Queens. KARI and DANNY sit. KARI is calm. DANNY is nervous.)

DANNY: She's late.

KARI: It's a tactic to make us nervous.

DANNY: Well it's working.

KARI: If they thought they could blow you off they wouldn't be meeting us. But the key to this thing going our way is to remain in the position of power. So we stay calm and collected. Okay?

DANNY: Okay.

(JAKE enters, spots DANNY, then approaches.)

JAKE: Danny Solis?

DANNY: Yeah.

JAKE: Hi. I'm Jake Colburn. I represent Miss Reed.

DANNY: Is she coming?

JAKE: Sadly she couldn't make it but she does send her regards. *(Seeing* KARI*)* And is this your friend?

*(*KARI *stands.)*

KARI: I'm Mister Solis's manager. Kari River.

*(*KARI *extends a hand.* JAKE *shakes it cordially.)*

JAKE: I thought we agreed this was going to be informal.

DANNY: I just wanted someone here looking out for me.

JAKE: Of course. It's smart. *(Beat)* Before we begin can I get you two something?

KARI: We're fine. Can we get you something?

JAKE: I'm okay, but thank you. *(He sits.)* For the sake of not wasting time let's get down to brass tacks. This is for you.

*(*JAKE *takes out an envelope and puts it in front of* DANNY. *It looks like money.)*

DANNY: What is this? Money?

JAKE: It's a co-authoring agreement.

(As JAKE *speaks* KARI *opens the document and looks it over.)*

JAKE: Miss Reed fully understands your concern regarding the similarities between your song and her single, so as token of good faith she wants to offer you a co-writing credit which will be retroactive. Layman's terms- you get a cut from this point forward, in addition to anything earned since inception. Any questions?

KARI: Just a few.

JAKE: Sure.

KARI: Here in section H dash one it says that Danny— my client, needs to remove his song from any and all places where it appears online.

JAKE: And?

KARI: I'm not understanding why that's necessary.

JAKE: It makes the process more seamless.

KARI: For whom?

JAKE: All parties involved.

KARI: Not really, but we can get back to that. In section J dash two it states that the royalty split will be eighty-five fifteen in favor of Miss Reed?

JAKE: Given Miss Reed's status we feel the split is more than generous.

KARI: I disagree with that strongly.

(*A beat*)

JAKE: I'm receptive to a counter.

KARI: I think an equal split is fair.

JAKE: As in fifty-fifty?

KARI: That's what equal means.

JAKE: I'm sorry- what was your name again?

KARI: Kari River.

JAKE: I don't know how versed you are with royalty splits or what capacity you're serving as a manager, and to be honest I don't care. But fifty-fifty is in the next universe.

KARI: We're receptive to a counter.

JAKE: I'm authorized to push to eighty-twenty.

KARI: Forty-sixty.

JAKE: Seventy-thirty.

KARI: And if you want my client to remove his track from the internet it'll be another five.

(*A beat*)

JAKE: Great.

KARI: Good. In addition to receiving royalties on the single, my client wants make to a song with Miss Reed.

JAKE: A song.

KARI: A collaboration.

JAKE: Well, I'm sure she'll be flattered by the request.

KARI: Good. Because it needs to be on her upcoming album.

JAKE: What?

KARI: And given the nature of the events which have transpired, it's our position that you're obligated to grant us this request.

JAKE: Look. You just negotiated a thirty-five percent royalty cut to a song that's eleven on the Billboard music chart. That's a lot of money. So don't screw this up by getting greedy.

KARI: This has nothing to do with greed. My client wants exposure.

JAKE: And being listed as co-writer on the single he'll more than get it.

KARI: What my client wants is inclusion in the creative process.

JAKE: Well I want to be an astronaut but that doesn't mean I'm flying to the moon.

DANNY: Bro she stole my track!

KARI: Danny.

JAKE: Let me make something crystal clear. Miss Reed stole nothing. She created an original track which sounds incredibly similar to the one on your internet page. And that's the conversation we're having.

DANNY: Prove she didn't steal it.

JAKE: We don't have to. See that's how this works. You make the accusation, you have to back it up with hard proof.

DANNY: We've got that.

JAKE: Oh, you mean your song that's online and time marked? Do you know how easy it is to alter a time mark? Matter of fact how do I know that that isn't what you did? Maybe we should be the ones coming after you.

DANNY: Dude that's a bunch of—

KARI: Danny. Well I have to hand it to you Mister *(?)*

JAKE: Colburn.

KARI: I'm sure most people are intimidated by you. But I'm not. And I'm not going to sit here and let you bescumber us a second longer. Now do you agree to the terms I've laid out or not?

JAKE: No.

KARI: Two songs.

JAKE: What?

KARI: The old deal is dead. The new deal is we get two songs. You want to keep going?

DANNY: Okay, what happened to calm?

KARI: Calm went out the window the minute this guy started treating me like a little girl.

DANNY: Well lets just chill a sec.

JAKE: I suggest you listen to your client.

KARI: Three songs.

JAKE: I'm leaving. Don't contact me again.

(JAKE *stands and starts to walk away.*)

KARI: We'll go to every news outlet in the city with our evidence and the public decides what's what for themselves

(JAKE *walks back over.*)

JAKE: You do that and every lawyer at the label's disposal will descend on you like a swarm of locusts.

KARI: My father owns fourteen percent of Queens. He has more lawyers than you could ever count. So you want to go down that road? Let's do it.

Scene 6

(*Later that night. The hotel room in Manhattan.* RYAN *stands,* JAKE *sits, holding a glass of whiskey.*)

RYAN: You said you were going to fix this.

JAKE: Ryan—

RYAN: And not only did you not, but now I'm supposed to collaborate with someone who I've never met for my album?! I mean you pride yourself on being this amazing manager. But if you were, this would be managed!

JAKE: Ryan I did not create this situation.

RYAN: You were supposed to make it go away.

JAKE: I'm not a fucking magician.

RYAN: I'm not asking you to be a magician. I'm asking you to do what you say you're going to do.

JAKE: The kid wasn't alone.

RYAN: Who was he with?

JAKE: His manager.

RYAN: Did you know he had a manager?

JAKE: I did not.

RYAN: So you weren't prepared.

JAKE: Ryan you should be thanking me.

RYAN: Why?

JAKE: They were demanding multiple songs for the album.

RYAN: They weren't supposed to get any! And let's talk about the single. They're getting thirty five percent?!

JAKE: You stole the song!

RYAN: The only reason it's getting any exposure is because my name's on it!!

JAKE: And a year ago you were playing shit hole clubs.

RYAN: Okay that's it you're fired.

JAKE: What?

RYAN: Effective immediately.

JAKE: You can't fire me.

RYAN: You work for me.

JAKE: Ryan without me you're fucked.

RYAN: Apparently I'm fucked no matter what! I mean Jesus, my heart's racing, I feel dizzy.

(RYAN *starts to hyperventilate.* JAKE *goes to her.*)

JAKE: Okay. Relax. Calm down. Breathe.

(RYAN *looks at* JAKE *like "really?" He backs off. She starts to calm down.*)

JAKE: Better?

(RYAN *nods.*)

JAKE: See? This is what happens when you Google yourself. Now would you like to hear the plan?

RYAN: There's a plan?

JAKE: Are you kidding me?

RYAN: What?

JAKE: You're in need of material. You're blocked. The kid's talented and has a good sound that can help you reach a bigger audience across genres. So we rent a studio, the two of you go in for a few sessions, make some songs. The kid gets locked into an N D A, you walk away owning everything. Worst case you find some inspiration. Best case you've got another hit single.

RYAN: I'm capable of writing a hit by myself.

JAKE: I know. But sometimes we all need help.

RYAN: So I'm using him?

JAKE: Look, I get it. But before you go feeling too bad, keep in mind the kid is trying to use you too. Also his manager was going to the press.

RYAN: I just didn't see myself ever being in this position.

JAKE: Well if it makes it easier you're definitely not the first. Now get some sleep. Your schedule is about to get twice as busy.

RYAN: You know, it would have been nice if you'd of just told me there was a plan instead of coming in here and scaring the shit out of me.

JAKE: You needed to be scared. People will go to extraordinary lengths to get a piece of you. Don't make it easy for them. *(He exits.)*

Scene 7

(A day later. The apartment in Queens. DANNY is sitting listening to the single on his phone. KARI is focused on the computer.)

DANNY: I can't believe this is happening. I mean that guy was coming at us, then we were coming at him. Then you dropped that shit about your dad?

KARI: That was a bluff.

DANNY: All I know is I'm collaborating with RYAN REED.

KARI: I thought you thought she sucks.

DANNY: I do. But this is next level shit. Professional studio, professional equipment. I bet we even have an engineer.

KARI: Danny slow down I'm not done reading the contract.

DANNY: But they sent the contract! Which means this is happening.

KARI: It's not that simple. There's tons of provisions, sub provisions—

DANNY: Yeah it's a contract.

KARI: They're trying to trap us. Which is why you need a lawyer to look this over.

DANNY: A lawyer?

KARI: I'll put out feelers to entertainment lawyers.

DANNY: Kari I'm supposed to be starting this in two days. I don't have time to fuck around with lawyers.

KARI: You owe it to yourself to do this right.

DANNY: I will.

KARI: You don't even know what's in here.

DANNY: Then tell me.

KARI: For starters, you won't own anything and you won't have any creative control.

DANNY: Do I get credit?

KARI: A development credit.

DANNY: Do I get paid?

KARI: You receive a fee plus a small royalty if it gets published.

DANNY: I'm good with that.

KARI: Danny at the very least you should have some say in what goes on.

DANNY: I want that too but I can make it work. Was there anything else?

KARI: There's a built in non-disclosure that prohibits you from talking about the collaboration or the single with anyone. And if you do she can sue you for up to five million dollars.

DANNY: Alright, so I won't say shit to anyone and Ryan and I will make a hit song and then it will be all good.

KARI: Danny do you really think they're going to just hand this to you?

DANNY: They're not handing me shit. I earned this.

KARI: Danny.

DANNY: You think I haven't?

KARI: What I'm saying is that guy caved way too easy.

DANNY: You worked his ass over.

KARI: He has a record label behind him. If he wanted to he could destroy us.

DANNY: So what? Now you're scared?

KARI: Yes I'm feeling trepidation. If we don't do this exactly right it's gonna go away.

DANNY: And if we piss them off with this back and forth shit it'll go away. Now was there anything else?

KARI: You have four three-hour sessions to work together.

DANNY: Cool.

KARI: That seems like a really short amount of time.

DANNY: I normally make tracks in less than half that.

KARI: Two days ago you were working at a taco restaurant!

DANNY: Fuck you, so what?!

KARI: So you're being so naive it's making my brain twitch!

DANNY: You think I don't get that this is a bad deal? Because yes, it's clearly not great. But this could be my only chance to make it happen and I'm not lettin' it slip. So gimme that shit before these dudes change their minds. *(He takes the computer. He's not immediately sure what needs to be done.)*

KARI: Just needs an E signature on each page.

(DANNY begins going through the contract.)

KARI: There's something I need to talk to you about.

DANNY: What's up?

KARI: My dad is selling this building.

DANNY: What?

KARI: Some developer guy offered him a bunch of money and he took it.

DANNY: When's he selling?

KARI: Soon.

DANNY: Okay. Cool.

KARI: Cool?

DANNY: I mean not cool. That shit sucks. I'm just saying I'm getting thirty five percent and the money's gonna be coming in.

KARI: Do you think it would be possible to get some money for helping you? I mean I hate to ask, it's just I'm getting less shifts at the candle store and the building—

DANNY: You don't have to explain. What'd you have in mind?

KARI: Ten percent of whatever you get is pretty standard.

DANNY: Boom. Done.

(DANNY *and* KARI *do a handshake.*)

KARI: Thank you.

DANNY: (*Pressing a button on the keypad.*) Sent. (*He closes the computer and gets up.*) I'll see you later alright?

KARI: Where are you going?

DANNY: If I start this shit in two days I gotta get to work.

(DANNY *exits. Lights fade.*)

Scene 8

(*We see* TOMMY, *a guy in his 50s who bears a resemblance to* DANNY. *He takes out a cell phone, dials a number, makes a call.*)

(FELICIA *enters in another part of the playing space. We hear her phone go off. She takes it out, looks at it, doesn't answer.*)

(*It goes to voice mail.*)

TOMMY: Hey honey, it's dad. Just calling, again. Hope you're doing okay. Please give me a call. (*He hangs up, then exits.*)

(FELICIA *receives the voice mail. She looks at her phone, deletes it, exits.*)

Scene 9

(A day later. Interior hallway)

RYAN: You Danny?

DANNY: Yeah. Nice to meet you.

RYAN: You're late. By fifteen minutes. Not a great first impression.

DANNY: I know, but the "E" was all sorts of fucked up and this building totally blends in. I walked up and down this block three times just trying to find it.

RYAN: It's intentionally meant to be low profile.

DANNY: Yeah, I know. All the people who've recorded here?

RYAN: Before we get started I want to lay down some ground rules.

DANNY: Alright.

RYAN: First off, I've got an incredibly busy schedule and I'm not going to wait around for you ever again. So if I show up and you're not here I'm leaving.

DANNY: From now on I'll be on time.

RYAN: Do you have music for today?

DANNY: Yeah.

RYAN: Great. Moving forward your role in this is to bring four ideas to each session. And if I don't like the idea, it's dead. Got it? Good. Also I really need you coming in here not high.

DANNY: I'm not high.

RYAN: You reek like weed.

DANNY: It was just this dude on the street I was walking behind.

RYAN: Just don't do it, okay?

DANNY: Look, I know that I don't know you and you don't know me, but you don't need to be all whatever. I'm here to make something dope and I'm not trying to waste time.

RYAN: Then we should probably get started.

DANNY: Sounds good.

RYAN: Great. We're in Room B.

(RYAN, *motioning to a room we don't see. A beat as* DANNY *looks at it.*)

RYAN: What?

DANNY: That shit is tiny.

RYAN: It's a composer's room. *(Beat)* Welcome to the big leagues.

(RYAN *goes into the studio. For a moment* DANNY *remains. He exhales then enters the room.*)

Scene 10

(*Several days later. The interior of the studio. There's several pieces of equipment set up—a small sound board, a keyboard, and two laptop computers which are both open.* DANNY *is playing* RYAN *a beat. It's pretty catchy. He is nodding his head into it.*)

RYAN: Nope.

(DANNY *stops the beat.*)

DANNY: Okay what is the issue?

RYAN: What do you mean?

DANNY: For two sessions now I've been playing you nothing but dope beats, and you're not even giving my stuff a chance.

RYAN: You just played me a beat that sounded like 80′ Madonna. And before that you played one with Avril Lavigne's voice sampled in it.

DANNY: So?

RYAN: Those are super weird references and I don't know what to make with that!

DANNY: Dude I don't even understand how you make music. The idea is to work together. To tweak shit. To experiment. To jam!

RYAN: To jam?

DANNY: I fuckin love jamming!

RYAN: Wow.

DANNY: You don't love jamming??

RYAN: This isn't a garage.

DANNY: You are like the most un-fun person I've ever met.

RYAN: I'm being professional.

DANNY: Dude for real—do you even enjoy doing this?

RYAN: I love what I do.

DANNY: Coulda fooled me. You're like so up in your own head and freaked out. Enjoy the process!

RYAN: The process?

DANNY: Fuck yeah the process! That's how you get to the soul! The core, the heart.

RYAN: You know, for a DJ you sure think you know a lot about writing songs.

DANNY: Fuck you I'm a musician.

RYAN: Musicians play instruments.

DANNY: I do play an instrument.

RYAN: And what instrument is that?

DANNY: The computer.

RYAN: I'm talking about a real instrument.

DANNY: You want a real instrument?

(DANNY *goes to the keyboard and starts to play a song. He is a really good pianist. This catches* RYAN *off guard.*)

RYAN: If you can play piano like that, what are you doing messing around on a computer?

DANNY: Because a computer can make music as good or better than any other shit. And if you're so hot on real instruments how come all your recent shit sounds like it came out of a computer?

RYAN: My music has always had electronic elements.

DANNY: Yeah I know. I looked you up and your shit used to be gritty and raw. You used to sing about spending the night in jail. But now you sing about breaking up with dudes.

RYAN: I evolved as an artist.

DANNY: Evolved or sold out?

RYAN: I softened my edge to appeal to a larger audience.

DANNY: I'm pretty sure that's the definition of selling out.

RYAN: You say that shit to me again and I'll punch you in the face. (*A beat, then she goes to the sound board and prepares to resume working.*)

DANNY: You're from Oklahoma right?

RYAN: Just outside of Tulsa.

DANNY: What's that shit like?

RYAN: When I was eighteen I moved to Detroit and haven't looked back since.

DANNY: Cool. My story is kinda similar, I guess.

RYAN: So who taught you to play?

DANNY: My pop was a pro musician.

RYAN: That's cool. You two close?

DANNY: Nah, I haven't seen him for a few years.

RYAN: He's not around anymore?

DANNY: He bounced when I was younger to go out West and make it. Scored a record deal. The shit fell apart. Last I heard he was back out this way trying to start over.

RYAN: That sucks. (She picks up a guitar and starts to fiddle with notes.)

DANNY: (Beat) So look, how did things happen for you?

RYAN: Like how did I get "discovered"?

DANNY: Yeah. I mean what? Did you send someone a demo tape?

RYAN: A demo tape?

DANNY: You know what I'm saying.

RYAN: Jake saw one of my online videos, contacted me, introduced me to people, I got a recording contract.

DANNY: That's amazing.

RYAN: When the label signed me, I thought it was the answer to everything. And then my producer asks me to alter something in my song, but the way he asks I know he's not asking. The change seems little so I agree. And then he asks for another. And another. And before I know it I don't know what the fuck I'm even making and I'm copying songs.

DANNY: Ah… You said it.

RYAN: Fuck you.

(Beat)

DANNY: Maybe all this shit happened cause it's the way things were meant to happen.

RYAN: Like it was fate that I stole your song?

DANNY: "Like they say,

God works in a mysterious way."

RYAN: We're quoting Gang Starr now?

DANNY: What you know about Gang Starr?

RYAN: Because I'm a white girl I can't know rap?

(A moment between DANNY *and* RYAN*)*

DANNY: Look, I got this beat I started last night. It's hard, but you wanna hear it?

RYAN: Okay. Yeah.

*(*DANNY *cues up a beat. It's a catchy drum track with electronic notes in it. She listens to it a moment, then—)*

RYAN: Can you slow it down?

*(*DANNY *presses stop, does some things on his computer, then presses play and the beat is slower. After a moment—)*

RYAN: Can you take out those Mario sounds?

*(*DANNY *gives her a little look, then presses stop, does some things on his computer, then presses start. All the remains is the slowed down drum track.* RYAN *starts to play to the beat. He goes to the keys and starts to play. They twiddle around a bit, until he discovers a note arrangement that she likes.)*

RYAN: That's cool. Can you put that in your— *(Motions to computer)*?

DANNY: Yeah.

*(*DANNY *goes to his computer and takes several moments putting the notes he just played on the keys into the program as* RYAN *continues to work on the chord progression. When he's done he presses play and a bass line matching what he played on the keys is now part of the beat.)*

RYAN: Cool. What else you got?

(*After a moment of thought, DANNY turns down the beat a bit and spits a freestyle. Part way through RYAN strums along with it.*)

(*She starts to strum a bridge and comes up with lyrics on the spot.*)

(*DANNY goes back to the keys and they begin to jam and it's awesome. It picks up intensity and is filled with joy. This is the first time we've seen RYAN smile.*)

(*When they are done they look at each other like "kinda rough but that was definitely cool".*)

(*Lights out.*)

Scene 11

(*Two days later. The Queens apartment. DANNY sits working on something last minute while on the phone.*)

DANNY: (*Into phone*) Dude come on. Felicia I'm not disowning anyone, I'm just busy. I can't get into it. Well I picked up the phone didn't I? Look I'm running late I gotta go. Later. I said later. (*He hangs up.*)

(*KARI enters.*)

KARI: Hey.

DANNY: Hey. There any cereal left?

KARI: Sorry.

DANNY: Shit. I'm starving and I gotta be in mid-town in an hour.

KARI: You just get up?

DANNY: Sorta. Aren't you supposed to be at work?

KARI: Not on today.

DANNY: Cool.

KARI: So how's everything going with Ryan??

DANNY: *(Occupied)* You know.

KARI: I don't. Which is why I'm asking.

DANNY: *(Momentarily stopping what he's doing)* Dude it's frickin' awesome!

KARI: Yeah?

DANNY: Yeah. I mean the room we're in has these panels on the ceiling to bounce acoustics and the chairs we sit on are like specially designed to hit pressure points in your back. And when you walk into the building there's this receptionist sitting there like a total hardass with these neck tattoos and shit and the first day I go in there and she's like "can I help you," but she says it in a tone like she thinks I'm just some dude who wandered in off the street. And I'm like "I'm Danny Solis and I'm here to work with Ryan Reed." And she's like "are you on the list?" And I'm all like fuuuck cause I have no idea if I'm on the list but I tell her that I am so she looks at the list and then she's like "Thank you Mister Solis. Miss Reed is waiting for you on the third floor." And I'm like "Thanks," but on the inside I was like WHAHHHHHHH.

KARI: That's incredible.

DANNY: For real. I've never been a "mister" before. *(He resumes finishing up what he's working on.)*

KARI: So how's working with Ryan?

DANNY: Way better than I thought it'd be.

KARI: Cool. You got something put together?

DANNY: I don't wanna get ahead of myself, but I think we might have something.

KARI: Awesome. Can I hear it?

DANNY: I'd say yes, but I promised Ryan I wouldn't share anything.

KARI: Danny I always listen to your new stuff.

DANNY: This is different

KARI: How?

DANNY: For starters there's this N D A.

KARI: The N D A I warned you not to sign that you signed anyway?

DANNY: Dude it's all good.

KARI: We've barely spoken since you started this thing and now you're making me interrogate you to find out what's going on with Ryan. It's like I'm in the rear view mirror, man.

DANNY: Kari you're not in the rear view mirror. You're like right there in the front mirror.

KARI: The front mirror is called the rear view mirror.

DANNY: That's not what I meant. You're definitely part of this. I'm just busy as hell and I really gotta finish this.

KARI: I'm gonna come to the studio with you.

DANNY: What, like right now?

KARI: *(Getting their bag)* I've never seen one and the way you describe it, it sounds cool.

DANNY: I mean it's not that great. It's a really small room. There's barely enough room for two chairs.

KARI: I don't want to stay. I just want to see it.

DANNY: I don't know that you can.

KARI: Why not?

DANNY: You gotta be on the list.

KARI: So get me on the list.

DANNY: How?

KARI: Talk to Ryan.

DANNY: And say what?

KARI: How about— "My manager wants to see our work space to make sure it's up to the standards of our agreement."

DANNY: You seriously expect me to say that shit to her?

KARI: It's an example.

DANNY: Kari why do you care? You're getting yours.

KARI: Excuse me?

DANNY: You're taken care of. You're getting paid. *(He starts putting his computer and headphones in backpack.)*

KARI: This isn't just about money for me. It's about being part of something with a friend. And seeing how meeting with Ryan's people was my idea I don't think wanting to see your studio is an unreasonable request.

DANNY: Fine you want to see the fucking studio lets go. *(He gets up and heads to door.)*

KARI: Don't bite my head off.

DANNY: I'm not, I just got way more important shit to worry about than sneaking you into the studio just so you can feel like you're part of this!! But if it's really that important to you—

KARI: That's okay.

DANNY: Kari you literally just said you wanted to—

KARI: I'm busy today. But thanks. *(Starts looking at their phone)*

DANNY: Look I really gotta get going. Hey we're good right? Right?

KARI: Did you say something?

DANNY: Just that I'll see you later. *(He exits.)*

Scene 12

(Later that day. The recording studio. RYAN *is strumming her guitar.)*

RYAN:
Tell me how I oughta dress
Fuck you
Tell me what I oughta say
Fuck you
Tell me how I oughta act
Fuck you
Fuck you I'm not your girl.

*(*JAKE *enters.* RYAN *stops playing.)*

JAKE: Catchy but doubtful it'll get radio play.

RYAN: What are you doing here?

JAKE: I wanted to go over some things.

RYAN: In person?

JAKE: Where's Danny?

RYAN: Not here yet.

JAKE: He's late.

RYAN: It's all good. So what's up?

JAKE: Tomorrow we need to go to L A.

RYAN: Why?

JAKE: The label needs you to do some on camera interviews. Two days at the most.

RYAN: What time are we leaving?

JAKE: I booked a six A M.

*(*JAKE, *off* RYAN's *look:)*

JAKE: Relax, you're flying first class, you can sleep on the plane.

RYAN: So now you're just buying first class plane tickets without my okay.

JAKE: I wasn't aware I needed it.

RYAN: I'm paying for it.

JAKE: So you want to travel by bus?

(Beat)

RYAN: Anything else?

JAKE: I heard your new demo.

RYAN: What?

JAKE: The one you sent to the label last night that sounds like you singing over an indie hip hop beat.

RYAN: Why'd they send it to you?

JAKE: Why'd you send it to them?

RYAN: I wanted their thoughts.

JAKE: Ryan anytime you make something new I need to hear it first.

RYAN: Whatever.

JAKE: No not whatever. That's our agreement.

RYAN: They said they liked it. *(Beat)* Look, since you're here there some things we need to discuss.

JAKE: Sure.

RYAN: I've decided to make some changes.

JAKE: Meaning?

RYAN: As of today I'm done making any concessions to Bob. From now on we do things my way and that's it. Also I want you to tear up Danny's contract and make one that's not going to fuck him over.

JAKE: I ask this not as your manager but as someone who genuinely cares about you. Are you on drugs?

RYAN: Excuse me?

JAKE: It's fine if you are. I spent the eighties and nineties high as shit.

RYAN: I'm not on drugs. Now I've told you what I want. Get it done.

JAKE: May I talk now?

RYAN: What.

JAKE: I guess I'm just curious as to what changed between last week and now. Because last week we had a rock solid plan on how to contain this situation, and now you seem intent on blowing everything to shit, and I'm a little confused about that.

RYAN: That's exactly the problem.

JAKE: My confusion?

RYAN: Your inability to understand where I'm coming from.

JAKE: Okay so tell me.

RYAN: I want to make music that is true to me. But all I do is get pushed around by a producer who wants to make my songs sound like they should be in a car commercial.

JAKE: You know how much money you can make having your songs in a car commercial?

RYAN: Oh Jesus Christ.

JAKE: Yes, Jesus Christ welcome to the music business. You make commercial hits now so you can make fuck you songs later. The demo you sent the label doesn't work on any level.

RYAN: They said they liked it a lot.

JAKE: They were being sarcastic. They thought you sent it to them as a joke. And thank God they did because had they thought you were being serious we'd have a major problem.

RYAN: I get that the song is kinda different.

JAKE: The song isn't kinda different. The song is complete fucking garbage.

RYAN: I don't see it that way.

JAKE: And that scares the shit out of me because you clearly don't understand what we're trying to do here. *(Beat)* Tell me what I have to do to get through to you. Do I have to speak louder? Do I need to jump up and down and clap? How do I get you to see the light!?

(DANNY enters.)

DANNY: Dude sorry I'm late! The E was a frickin' disaster. *(Seeing JAKE and giving him a little nod)* Oh hey what up man?

JAKE: Well, have a great session. *(To DANNY)* Ryan asked me to tear up your contract. *(To RYAN)* See you in the morning.

(JAKE exits. A beat)

DANNY: What's he talking about?

RYAN: It's complicated.

DANNY: You want him to tear up my contract?

RYAN: For a better one. You're being exploited and I feel shitty.

DANNY: Hell yeah! Now we got the freedom to just go wild! *(Sensing something wrong)* What's up?

RYAN: Jake heard the demo we made.

DANNY: I thought we agreed we weren't going to share it.

RYAN: I wanted to get some outside thoughts.

DANNY: So what'd Jake think?

RYAN: That it's garbage.

DANNY: Well fuck you too, Jake.

RYAN: No, not fuck him. He's never been wrong about a song.

DANNY: Then whatever. I've got tons of other ideas.

RYAN: We don't need tons of ideas! We need to make a song that's NOT FUCKING GARBAGE. *(Beat. Then softer)* Look, tomorrow I need to head to LA for a few days.

DANNY: What for?

RYAN: Promotional stuff. I leave really early and I could use some rest. So maybe we should just pick things up when I get back.

DANNY: I'm gonna make this happen. This is my everything and I'm not going to lose it.

RYAN: I'll see you when I get back. *(She exits.)*

Scene 13

(A day later. A studio apartment. DANNY, *wearing a backpack, stands with* TOMMY.*)*

TOMMY: Daniel.

DANNY: Pop.

(DANNY and TOMMY look at each other a few moments.

TOMMY: Wow. Look at you. You're all, grown up.

DANNY: I am.

TOMMY: Come on. Don't just stand there. Give me a hug.

(After a moment DANNY *enters and he and* TOMMY *briefly hug.)*

TOMMY: Damn! You're diesel! You lifting weights?

DANNY: Okay, easy.

TOMMY: I'm just messing. Hey! You hungry?

DANNY: No.

TOMMY: You sure? There's a decent spot around the corner. I'm buying.

DANNY: I'm cool. But thanks.

(For a beat neither DANNY nor TOMMY know what to say. Then—)

DANNY: So. This place is, nice.

TOMMY: No it ain't.

DANNY: No. It ain't.

TOMMY: Truth is, it kills me living up in here. But, you know. I'm doin' what I have to. Workin'. Savin' up. So I can get a real pad.

DANNY: You planning on sticking around then?

TOMMY: Well, yeah. This is where I'm from.

DANNY: I know. I just figured after everything…

TOMMY: It's cool. I get it. *(Beat)* So how you been Danny?

DANNY: You know.

TOMMY: Actually I don't. Which is why I'm asking. You graduate high school?

DANNY: Yeah.

TOMMY: Great! You in college?

DANNY: Not at the moment.

TOMMY: So then what? You gotta a job? You gotta girl? You gotta kid?

DANNY: A kid?

TOMMY: When I was your age your ma was pregnant with Felicia.

DANNY: Look I'm not trying to play catch up right now.

TOMMY: Well excuse me for being curious but prior to yesterday I haven't spoken to you in two fuckin' years! *(A moment to calm down.)* I can't tell you how grateful I am that you reached out. I've been looking for a way to reconnect but I didn't have your number. And your sister? She won't pick up the phone.

DANNY: You've been callin' her?

TOMMY: Ever since I got back. I know it won't happen overnight, but I want to try and be part of both your lives again.

DANNY: Pop you don't have to say that.

TOMMY: Yes I do, because I mean it.

DANNY: Well I didn't come here for some big reconciliation.

TOMMY: So why did you?

DANNY: I need your help with a situation.

TOMMY: You in trouble?

DANNY: It's got to do with my music.

TOMMY: You still keeping up with that?

DANNY: Every single day.

TOMMY: Last time I spoke to your ma she said she was gonna make you give that up.

DANNY: Which is why I moved out.

TOMMY: What do you mean you moved out?

DANNY: Mom wouldn't stop with the negativity and I can't be around that anymore.

TOMMY: You staying at your sister's then?

DANNY: I'm actually not allowed over there.

TOMMY: Why not??

DANNY: Last time I was there I got in a scrap with Luis.

TOMMY: What did that jerkoff do now?

DANNY: It doesn't matter and right now I'm staying with a friend and it's all good.

(Beat)

TOMMY: So tell me about this situation.

DANNY: So basically I got hooked up with this big time singer who really digs my shit, and now I'm doing a collaboration with them for their upcoming album.

TOMMY: So how big time are they?

DANNY: Big. Time.

TOMMY: Danny! That's incredible, man! So who's the singer?

DANNY: I can't say.

TOMMY: Why not?

DANNY: Cause there's an N D A that's part of the agreement.

TOMMY: So what do you need me for?

DANNY: Things aren't going as well with the creative process as I want. So look I brought my computer with me, and I know you hate hip hop, but I was wondering if I could run some of my ideas by you.

TOMMY: Why?

DANNY: You've been at the top level and you know what it takes.

TOMMY: I never made things happen.

DANNY: But you got there.

TOMMY: Yes, Danny, I did. And then one day a label exec comes in the studio tellin' me I'm not playing to the strength of my sound. And when I refused to make changes I got dropped.

DANNY: I know you got a raw deal.

TOMMY: I didn't get a raw deal. I got fucked! And you're asking me for career advice??

DANNY: Yes!!

TOMMY: Okay. Walk the fuck away while you can. Because all that's gonna happen is you're gonna get robbed, cheated or fucked. Now drop this shit before I have a damn heart attack!

(A long beat)

DANNY: You get that it wasn't easy for me to come here, right? I mean I haven't seen your ass since you took off and before that you were around barely ever.

TOMMY: The last thing I need right now is your guilt trip.

DANNY: I'm telling you it's crazy for me to be here!! *(Beat)* Look, for a long time I've resented the fuck out of you for leaving. But I get it. You were going after your dream, just like how I am now. Pop I got a real shot at making it, and seeing as how you're the motherfucker who taught me everything I know, you can help get me there.

TOMMY: You don't understand what you're asking.

DANNY: Pop—

TOMMY: I haven't picked up a guitar in years. I don't even have one! I can't even listen the radio anymore because the shit's too painful!

DANNY: Dude this isn't about you! *(Beat)* You say you want to be my dad again? Here's your chance.

TOMMY: I've put that part of my life to bed. Please respect that.

DANNY: Cool. Great seeing you, pop. *(He gets up and starts to exit.)*

TOMMY: Danny hold up. I'm not saying it's gonna help, but if you wanna run some of your stuff by me, maybe I can show you some things.

DANNY: For real?

TOMMY: For real.

Scene 14

(The next evening. FELICIA *is standing outside her hospital in scrubs texting during a break.)*

*(*TOMMY *enters, holding a box wrapped in wrapping paper.)*

TOMMY: Excuse me miss? Can you point me towards the emergency room?

*(*FELICIA *sees* TOMMY.*)*

TOMMY: Hey sweetie. How are you? You look great. Professional. I mean you are. And this hospital is really something. Not like the one in our old neighborhood. Remember that place?

FELICIA: What are you doing here?

TOMMY: I'm tired of leaving voice mails.

FELICIA: How do you know I work here?

TOMMY: I called your house, little Anthony picked up, told me where you were. I brought you something. *(He holds up the box.)* It's a toy drum. For the twins. I wanted to get two, but I'm kinda tight on money and you know, they can share.

*(*FELICIA *turns to go.)*

TOMMY: Felish hold up. Can you just gimme a sec?

FELICIA: Why?

TOMMY: I'm your dad.

FELICIA: *(Are you serious?)* Really?

TOMMY: Okay then how about because it took me nearly an hour and two transfers to get here.

FELICIA: What do you want?

TOMMY: To try and make things right between us.

FELICIA: You can't.

TOMMY: I know I fucked up, but I'm not the villain I've been made me out to be.

FELICIA: Here we go.

TOMMY: Your mother knew who I was and what I was going after when she married me, and the minute I started getting success—

FELICIA: So it's her fault you treated her like shit and abandoned our family?

TOMMY: I didn't abandon anyone.

FELICIA: Packing a bag and leaving in the middle of the night wasn't abandoning your family?

TOMMY: All due respect you don't know how things went down because you were shacked up with mister rent-a-cop.

FELICIA: Luis is a highly trained security—

TOMMY: —The point is, I tried to make things work. I wanted your mother and Danny to come out with me, but your mother wouldn't even hear it.

FELICIA: What was she supposed to do? Go out there with no job or support system and watch you fuck groupies?

TOMMY: I wasn't fucking groupies!

FELICIA: So the time I called and that girl answered sounding all drunk—

TOMMY: Like I said, that was an intern, from the studio, messing with my phone—

FELICIA: You've got an excuse for everything.

TOMMY: I'm telling you what happened. And I'm not gonna feel bad about going West cause it was better than staying here, giving up my music and resenting all of you the rest of my life.

FELICIA: I'm sorry, is this you trying to win me back?

TOMMY: I'm being honest.

FELICIA: Honesty's not your best look. But since we're being honest, I'm glad you left cause it paved the way for a real man to step in.

TOMMY: Who? Mister Jesus army man?

FELICIA: His name is Ron and he was a Marine. And you wanna know why mom married him? Cause he's the opposite of you.

TOMMY: Felicia I know wasn't a good father. I'm owning that. But if Danny's willing to give me another chance, you should be too.

FELICIA: What are you talking about?

TOMMY: He reached out.

FELICIA: Why?

TOMMY: He needed help with a situation.

FELICIA: What situation?

TOMMY: This song he's writing with a big time singer.

FELICIA: I have no idea what you're talking about.

TOMMY: Clearly. And what's up with him not being allowed over at your house? He's having a hard time and it's your responsibility to look out for him.

FELICIA: You're lecturing me about responsibility??

(A beat)

TOMMY: I've got this memory. It's from when you were little, before Danny was around. Saturday mornings when your mother was still at work, I'd wake you up, cook you breakfast—you liked pancakes with chocolate chips. Then we'd head over to the park and chill. Those times were the highlight of my week, cause it was me and you, and I miss that.

FELICIA: I'm glad you've got good memories. But you know what I remember? That everything was always about you. What you needed. And when you weren't getting what you thought you deserved, you came home, and took it out on us. I thank God Danny was young enough to not remember most of it, but things happened that I will never forget.

TOMMY: I'm not asking you to forget. I'm asking for the chance to show that I've changed.

FELICIA: You say you've changed? I'm happy for you. But I've moved on. Please don't contact me again.

(FELICIA *walks away.* TOMMY *stands there.*)

Scene 15

(*Next morning. Inside the apartment in Queens.* DANNY *is on the couch with his computer.* KARI *enters, sees him, then walks by him going to their bedroom.*)

DANNY: Where you been?

KARI: What do you mean?

DANNY: You didn't come home last night.

KARI: I've been out.

DANNY: Okay cool. Hey you gotta hear this track I made!

KARI: Is it the one from the other day?

DANNY: No. That one ended up sucking so I've been up all night working on something new.

KARI: Yeah I can tell. You're a mess right now.

DANNY: I'm fine. I'm just excited cause this is like the best shit I've done. Here. Listen.

KARI: No that's okay.

DANNY: Come on Kari!

KARI: Alright fine just play it. *(Comes over)*

DANNY: Use the phones.

(DANNY gives KARI the phones and hits play. KARI listens to the music for several moments. Though KARI nods to the beat, their face seems pained.)

DANNY: So?

KARI: It's good.

DANNY: Dude I play you the best shit I've ever made and you say it's "good"?

KARI: Okay fine it's the most prodigiously excellent beat I've ever heard are you happy now?

DANNY: Dude are you still pissed about the other day?

KARI: I'm tired of living in flux and having no purpose to my existence.

DANNY: If you feel that way then do something about it.

KARI: *(Takes off the phones)* I am. I'm moving to Taos to work at my aunt's hotel.

DANNY: Where the fuck is Taos?

KARI: Google it and find out. *(Gets up)*

DANNY: When are you leaving?

KARI: The day after tomorrow.

DANNY: Where am I supposed to go??

KARI: I don't know and I don't care. Ever since you moved in here you've treated me like I'm your life facilitator and I'm tired of it.

DANNY: Dude we're friends!

KARI: What does it mean to be someone's friend? Does it mean crashing at their place because you have nowhere else to go? No. It means talking to them about things that are real. Genuinely caring about what they're going through. It means having their back.

DANNY: Kari I do have your back!

KARI: Really? Because you don't know about anything going on in my life- how I quit my job or that I've been feeling completely alone, or even that I asked my dad if I could move back in and he told me I couldn't because I embarrass him.

DANNY: How is it possible that all of that is going on since the last time we talked?

KARI: It's been happening! And the reason you don't know is because you haven't asked.

DANNY: I'm fighting for my life here! I mean do you not get how important this is for me? Cause if I don't make this Ryan thing happen there's nothing else I can do.

KARI: Danny just stop!! I accept you for who you are— an incredibly selfish person. Now pack your shit and go.

(*A loud knock on the front door.* KARI *exits.*)

DANNY: Dude what the fuck?? (*He goes to the door and answers.*)

(FELICIA *is standing there.*)

DANNY: What are you doing here?

FELICIA: I need a word.

DANNY: It's not the best time.

FELICIA: I don't care.

DANNY: Okay. What's up?

FELICIA: You know exactly what's up.

DANNY: No I don't.

FELICIA: Take a guess who ambushed me at work last night?

DANNY: I don't know.

FELICIA: Dad. To tell me that he not only wants to reconnect, but that you saw him the other day.

DANNY: I had to talk to him about stuff.

FELICIA: About your music stuff? He told me all about that. How you're working with some big singer and you needed his help figuring it out.

DANNY: I did.

FELICIA: Out of all the people in the world, you go to him?

DANNY: He understands the situation cause he's been there, and I don't have to explain shit to you.

FELICIA: Actually you do because he called my house. My son picked up the phone and answered.

DANNY: What's the big deal?

FELICIA: I don't want him talking to my son! *(Beat)* Do you know what else he said? That it seemed like you were having a rough time and that I should look out for you.

DANNY: Maybe you should.

FELICIA: You think I don't?

DANNY: I feel like you could stand up for me more.

FELICIA: Tell me Danny. When do I ever not stand up for you?

DANNY: How about when you let your jerkoff husband kick me out of your house.

FELICIA: He had every right seeing how you broke his jaw.

DANNY: Saying what he said he's lucky I didn't break his neck.

FELICIA: What did he say that was so wrong?

DANNY: That he never wanted dad to be around your kids.

FELICIA: You know why Luis said that? Because he knows it's how I feel.

DANNY: You don't want dad around your kids like ever?

FELICIA: No Danny. Because all he's been to anyone is poison.

DANNY: That's not true.

FELICIA: So you're saying he's been a good dad?

DANNY: I'm saying I can see things from his perspective. And it's fucked up you didn't tell me he's been calling you.

FELICIA: So what? You want dad back in your life?

DANNY: I want the option instead of you controlling the shit for me.

FELICIA: Dad's a selfish fuck who's always done whatever he wanted regardless of who got hurt.

DANNY: I know he did shitty stuff and it was fucked up he left, but least the dude went for it. What the fuck have you ever done except settle?

FELICIA: So going to college, becoming an E R nurse, being a mother- to you that shit's settling?

DANNY: You used to have dreams.

FELICIA: I did. And guess what? I accomplished them.

DANNY: What you did is become salty and bitter. Just like ma.

FELICIA: So that's how you see me? How you see ma? Salty and bitter?

DANNY: Well aren't you?

FELICIA: (A beat) You know what, Danny? You are a grown man and you're free to do and say what you want. But if you let him, dad will hurt you. And when he does, it'll be no one's fault but your own.

(FELICIA turns and exits. During the argument KARI entered and was silently watching. DANNY sees them and exits to his room. After a moment he returns with his backpack and without looking at KARI he exits.)

Scene 16

(The next day. RYAN in a hotel room in Los Angeles. She's writing lyrics in her notebook. JAKE enters busy texting on his phone.)

RYAN: Do we have time to see the ocean before our flight?

JAKE: No.

RYAN: Jake come on man. It was my one request.

JAKE: (Puts phone away) Ryan I just had a meeting with your label. (A beat) They found out that you copied the single.

RYAN: Did you tell them?

JAKE: They were contacted by an attorney.

RYAN: Danny had a lawyer contact my label?

JAKE: Danny didn't write the song.

RYAN: …

JAKE: Sway is owned by a Thomas Solis who I'm guessing is his dad.

RYAN: No way.

JAKE: The original was recorded six years ago by a major label.

RYAN: My song's been out almost two weeks. So why did they wait til now to contact the label?

JAKE: Ryan we're dealing with theft of copyrighted material and I just spent an hour being screamed at by record execs who want to cancel your debut album!

RYAN: Are they going to?

JAKE: I convinced them not to. So now you're going back to New York, getting back in the studio, and this side project is over.

RYAN: You don't get to make that call.

JAKE: Ryan—

RYAN: I like working with him and I'm not stopping.

JAKE: You won't have time.

RYAN: I have two songs left to record and then the album is done.

JAKE: Actually you don't. While the label didn't like the track on the demo you sent them, they decided they love the hip hop direction. So they want to scrap everything and have you record new songs written by artists more familiar with the genre.

RYAN: You're fucking with me.

JAKE: No.

RYAN: You told them to shove it up their ass, right? Right?

JAKE: I agree with them.

RYAN: You told me you thought that demo was garbage.

JAKE: You are under contract with the second biggest label in the country.

RYAN: I'm still not singing other people's shit. I'm not doing it.

JAKE: Then the label's cancelling the album.

RYAN: Fine. Fuck them. I'll find another way.

JAKE: They're putting millions into this record. You think they're just going to let you go off?? *(She throws her notebook at the wall.)* You know what your problem is? You don't appreciate the gift you've been given. Do you know how many people would kill to possess even half of your musical ability? That at one point in my life I had ambitions of standing where you are now? But I wasn't good enough, and at the moment, neither are your songs. It's just a fact. Own it and move forward. *(Beat)* Ryan, you have the tools for greatness. You just have to walk through the door. *(Beat)* I'm going to the lobby. If you're not down in five I'll know your decision. *(He exits.)*

(RYAN stands motionless.)

Scene 17

(A day later. DANNY and RYAN in the recording studio.)

DANNY: So taking a breather was the right call cause while you were gone I came up with something.

RYAN: Danny.

DANNY: Now look, I'm not gonna set it up I just want you to listen.

RYAN: Danny.

DANNY: Also—keep in mind it's not close to done. I mean there's stuff that can be added and cut, but I think the idea is really—

RYAN: I know *Sway* isn't yours.

DANNY: What?

RYAN: The music belongs to your dad.

DANNY: I don't understand how you—

RYAN: His lawyer contacted my label.

DANNY: I can explain.

RYAN: Danny.

DANNY: It's not how you think it is and if you just let me—

RYAN: IT'S A SONG THAT WAS RECORDED BY A LABEL. If you think I'm pissed I'm not. I mean you saw a chance and you took it. In your spot I'd of done the same thing. Really I did the same thing.

DANNY: Look, forget *Sway*. I'm still me and you're still you. We can still make something original.

RYAN: What does being original even mean? Do you know why I got my record contract? Because the label thought I sounded like Taylor with more edge. I remember them saying that and at first I just wanted to spit in their faces, but why is it bad to sound like something that so many people love?

DANNY: So you're just gonna allow your producer to keep changing your shit?

RYAN: What I'm going to do is get there because I've worked too hard not to. I have to start being real about what I want. And I want the recognition. I want people to buy my music. I even want to move to L A.

DANNY: Dude fuck L A.

RYAN: You've never been to L A.

DANNY: I don't have to go there to know the shit sucks.

RYAN: L A. The only city people hate that they've never been to.

DANNY: Look, listen to my new track, and if you don't dig it never talk to me again.

RYAN: Danny.

DANNY: I swear to you on my life that it's—

(JAKE enters.)

JAKE: Ryan we should get going.

RYAN: Look, it was really nice meeting you.

(RYAN exits. JAKE takes an envelope out of his pocket.)

JAKE: Compensation for your time.

(JAKE gives the envelope to DANNY, then exits.)

Scene 18

(The next day. TOMMY's place. TOMMY is wearing new jeans and is sipping a celebratory glass of whiskey.)

TOMMY: I assume you're here about the song. *(Beat)* I was feeling so good after our talk, I paid your sister a visit. Bad idea. On the train home there was this guy playing music on his phone, and there it was. *Sway. (He takes out his phone and starts to play the single.)* It's amazing. I thought that song was a throw away. I guess you never know what's gonna hit.

DANNY: After everything that's happened in our family, how do you step in on me like this?

TOMMY: If anyone stepped in it's you. Taking something pure like *Sway* and turning it into hip hop bullshit?

DANNY: It's my interpretation. And I had every right.

TOMMY: Why is that?

DANNY: The song is mine.

TOMMY: Yours??

DANNY: That's right.

TOMMY: So why is my name on the copyright?

DANNY: Cause I was a minor and you told me for legal reasons—

TOMMY: Jesus Christ you're gonna pull that shit??

DANNY: So what? You saying that I wasn't part of it? Cause I was there pop, sitting at the keys coming up with the notes.

TOMMY: You were jamming with me on a song that I own the rights to!! And I had every right to know what the hell was going on!! So why didn't you tell me?

DANNY: I didn't want to risk my deal falling apart.

TOMMY: Bullshit! You didn't tell me because you wanted the fame and the glory all to yourself. And on top of that you had the balls to ask me for help? You little snake. Ready to fuck over whoever.

DANNY: Pop I swear to God I was gonna come to you when everything was finished and I was gonna cut you in and it coulda been like the old days when I was younger. But you ruined that and now it's fucked.

TOMMY: It was fucked from the start PAPA! Say I didn't do what I did. What'd you think was gonna happen? That you were gonna become some superstar? No Danny. One way or another you were gonna get fucked, so you know what? It might as well have come from me.

DANNY: I defended you, man. Felicia was saying all this shit and I stood up for you. But everything she said was true.

TOMMY: And what's that?

DANNY: That if I let you, you'd hurt me. And you did, pop. You hurt me worse than anyone ever has.

TOMMY: What about me? You don't think I'm hurting? That I can't remember the last time I wasn't hurting? I need something to hold onto. I need to know that outta all the shit I did, that there's at least one good thing. A thing that counts for something. Can you understand that?

DANNY: Honestly pop, I can. I don't know if I'll ever make it as a musician, but one thing I do know is I never want to become you ever. *(Beat)* Congratulations on the song. I'm happy it finally happened for you.

(DANNY exits. TOMMY sits alone.)

Scene 19

(The next day. The apartment in Queens. DANNY stands in the space. He puts an envelope on the table. KARI enters from their bedroom with a travel backpack.)

KARI: Hey.

DANNY: Hey…I left a few things behind. *(Beat)* So today's the day huh?

KARI: Yeah catching a train in a few hours.

DANNY: To Taos. Which after Googling I discovered is in New Mexico.

KARI: I'm kind of freaking out. I've never been west of New Jersey.

DANNY: So look. About the other day—

KARI: I shouldn't have freaked out like I did.

DANNY: No, lately I've been acting like a real dick.

KARI: Maybe. But you're under a lot of pressure with this Ryan thing.

DANNY: Actually that's done.

KARI: What?

DANNY: Yeah.

KARI: Why?

DANNY: It's complicated. *(Beat)* But it's not a total loss. I got four grand. *(Picks up the envelope)* So there's your cut.

KARI: Keep it.

DANNY: No you earned it.

KARI: *(Takes money)* Last night your sister came by. She told me that if I saw you to tell you that she could fix up her basement and you could live down there for as long as you needed.

DANNY: Yeah. I talked to her too, and it looks like I'm gonna be doing that.

KARI: That's great.

DANNY: Well I don't know if it's great…

KARI: It is. She really cares about you Danny. You're lucky to have that.
I really need to—

DANNY: Yeah.

KARI: You sticking around?

DANNY: For a sec. My sis is swinging by to pick me up.

KARI: Okay. *(Beat)* Take it easy, alright?

(DANNY and KARI do a handshake. KARI heads for the door.)

DANNY: Kari, you've been a real friend to me and you know, I don't have a lot of those. I'm sorry I haven't been one back.

(A beat)

KARI: That new track you played me the other day? Shit was seriously dope.

(KARI smirks at him, he smirks at KARI, then KARI's gone. DANNY is alone. He takes in the space then he turns and exits, returning with a shoebox. He puts down the box, sits and goes through the box, takes out a handheld tape deck and some cassette tapes. After looking through the tapes, he takes one out and puts it in the deck. He presses play.)

(It's an old recording of a jam session—random notes being played on a stand up piano and an guitar playing the chord progression of Sway. *The piano starts to play notes that sound somewhat similar to other notes in the song, then the piano plays the notes for the hook to* Sway.*)*

TOMMY'S VOICE: Hold up. What was that?

DANNY'S VOICE: Just some notes.

TOMMY'S VOICE: Play that again.

(The piano plays the notes. The guitar mimics.)

TOMMY'S VOICE: Show me those chords.

(The piano plays the chords. The guitar follows.)

TOMMY'S VOICE: Is that right?

(They both hook into the progression and begin to jam.)

TOMMY'S VOICE: Yeah Danny! That's it, man!

DANNY'S VOICE: Thanks pop.

(This is the original version of the song. Like in any jam session, where the musicians have found a good groove, the music picks up intensity and pace, becoming joyful, soulful and bright.)

(As DANNY *listens to the recording, we see something change in him. The recording ends. He looks at the tape deck. He presses stop, sitting in silence.)*

(Lights fade to black.)

END OF PLAY

www.ingramcontent.com/pod-product-compliance
Lightning Source LLC
Chambersburg PA
CBHW052217090426
42741CB00010B/2576